Monographic Journals of the Near East Afroasiatic Linguistics AAL 1/3 (March 1974)

EXTRINSIC ORDERING IN CLASSICAL ARABIC[1]

by

Robert Hetzron
University of California, Santa Barbara

One speaks of extrinsic ordering when the order of application of two rules must be specifically indicated and does not follow from a general principle. In Arabic the survival of a long vowel in a syllable made closed by a contraction may be a case of such ordering, though it may also be interpreted as an intrinsically ordered sequel of 'nonproductive — operative' rules. On the other hand, the incongruent agreement of numerals with the underlying singulars of the cooccurring plural nouns is definitely extrinsically ordered.

TABLE OF CONTENTS

---

[1] In preparing this article, I have largely profited from consultations on linguistic formalism with Dr. C.D. Johnson and on details of Arabic grammar with Dr. Charles Wendell. Let me express my gratitude to them. Discussions with Dr. John Callender and Dr. Theo Vennemann have also been useful. Even though they did not seem to sympathize with the position adopted in the paper, their cooperation is very much appreciated. I wish to thank Jeffrey Olliff for helping prepare the final draft. Part of a grant by the Academic Senate of the University of California at Santa Barbara has been used in preparing this manuscript. The Roman-numbered forms in Section 2 refer to verbal derivation in Arabic: II: Iterative, III: Conative or Applicative, etc. In Semitic, roots consist of consonantal skeletons combined with vocalic, and often also consonantal, patterns to form words. Arabic case-endings are transcribed superscript.

1. THE CONCEPT OF ORDER OF RULES

One of the great innovations of the generative-transformational school of linguistics has been that it has shown that those layers of linguistic expression which are understood by means of abstraction (and are not directly observable) can also be formalized in precise terms, and that the various layers can be related to one another through a finite number of exact rules. It follows from the concept of several layers that the rules leading from deeper layers upward to surface expressions must be, at least partly, ordered according to the depth of the layers involved. One rule is usually not sufficient for connecting deep (conceptual) structures to the (morphologically statable) surface structures. More than one rule must apply to the same segment, and some rules must apply before others.

Take any two rules, A and B, applying to the same segment. The order relation between them may be one of the following four types:

(1) (a) Neutrality when either A followed by B or B followed by A would yield the same results.[1] (A - B → c, B - A → c)

(b) Equivalent interchangeability when the order A - B does not yield exactly the same surface-results as B - A, but both are acceptable and are furthermore equivalent.[2] (A - B → c, B - A → d, c ∼ d)

(c) Unilateral applicability, when the order A - B is the only viable one, because either (i) A could not exist if it followed B,[3] or (ii) B could not exist if it preceded A.[4] (A - B → c, (i) B - *A, (ii) *B - A)

(d) Potential interchangeability, when the orders A - B and B - A (both theoretically possible) would not yield the same output, and only one of the possible orders is acceptable in a given language.[5] (A - B → c, B - A → *d)

---

[1] Take, for instance, the agreement imposed by the subject on the verb, and the tense-agreement (consecutio temporum, optional in American English) downgrading the tense of a clause that is the complement of a quotative verb in the past. It does not matter whether in "I said that they were ill" (from "I said: 'They are ill'") the past plural form of the verb has been obtained through subject-agreement + tense-agreement: BE → are → were, or through tense-agreement + subject-agreement: BE → was → were.

[2] E.g. (Koutsoudas 1972: 94, based on G. Lakoff): "Which of the men who hated Charley did he attack?" (Wh-fronting + Pronominalization) ∼ "Which of the men who hated him did Charley attack?" (Pronominalization + Wh-fronting).

[3] When B refers to a class that A is a part of, and alters it so that it would be no more eligible for A, cf. (3) below. Example: the "exceptional" plural formations in English man → men, child → children, sheep → sheep, etc., disjunctively followed by the rule that makes noun plurals an -s (with morphophonemic complications). If the second rule preceded, all nouns would get a plural in -s, and there would be no room for the "exceptional" formations. (cf. Hetzron 1972a.)

[4] When A provides all the proper input to B, e.g., in "I gave Charley money" (from "I gave money to Charley") the optional rule that moves Dative-complements to a position between the verb and the Accusative complement must necessarily precede the rule that realizes the Dative as zero (or, if someone prefers it, reduces 'to' to zero) in a position between a verb and an Accusative complement. Without the first rule, the second could have no application at all.

[5] For instance, in "Three men are coming" the subject-to-verb agreement must follow the pluralization of nouns after numerals. The other order is theoretically possible, but it would yield the ungrammatical construction *"Three men is coming."

Note that (1c, ii) is a case where the output of A supplies all the "raw material" for B, whereas if A only supplies part of the input for B, which could still apply without this specific source, we have an instance of (1d). Thus, coextensive supplying is unilateral, and partial supplying is potentially interchangeable. The first three cases, (1a), (1b), and (1c), can be considered unordered in the sense that the grammar need not mention order; it either follows from the situation (1c) or does not matter at all. Only (1d) is properly ordered, in the sense that a particular grammar has to indicate the order of application explicitly, to exclude the other theoretically possible order. Note that, here too, one of the possible orders is a more "natural," unmarked order (Kiparsky 1968: 200),[1] but in some cases the marked, less natural order is to be used.

The earlier literature on this topic distinguished between an Intrinsic ordering "which is simply a consequence of how rules are formulated" (Chomsky 1965: 223, fn. 6), also termed self-ordering which "can be determined entirely from the rules themselves" (Chafe 1968: 124), referring primarily to my (1c, ii), unilateral applicability with coextensive supplying, and an Extrinsic ordering (Chomsky 1965: 223, fn. 6) where the arrangement of the sequential application of rules does not follow from their formulation, nor is it indifferent to order, but the grammarian actually has to attach ordinal number-tags to his rules so as to indicate the order of application explicitly: my (1d). Clearly, the main point is that, having stated the existence of a set of rules in the grammar of a language, one finds that most rules are to apply whenever and wherever they encounter a representation meeting their structural description (1a-b-c, ii), but some rules are not that free to apply whenever they can, but are either regulated by a general principle to apply after another one (1c, i, where B has to "wait" till A has skimmed its share), or are, as part of the grammatical description, marked to apply after another one (1d), the extrinsic ordering. In other words, most rules apply whenever they can, some rules are "fair" and restrain themselves so as to justify the stated existence of another rule, and some have to be bridled by decree. The first two types are "natural" and the last, the extrinsically ordering type, is "arbitrary."

The adoption of the powerful device of "extrinsic ordering," the possibility of imposing an arbitrary order of application on rules, led to excesses. Exceptions to almost general rules, or restrictions, can often be explained historically by events that came to upset a regular, balanced situation, in a given domain. It was convenient for linguists to build the historical sequence of rules into the seemingly synchronical description of a language, by assuming that the old, original form is still the "underlying" one, and the actually attested form is the result of a derivation from this underlying shape through operative rules that reflect deposits of historical events, like the annual rings in a tree (cf. Chafe 1968: 116-7). Since, naturally, the historical sequence of the emergence of changes does not obey any principles of "intrinsic" or "natural" ordering, the concept of ad hoc, arbitrary (but empirically justified) extrinsic ordering is indispensable for this system.

It is, however, easy to see that these linguists have fallen into a trap. The psychology is understandable. A describer, whatever the discipline, has an "abhorrence of irregularity," and such a basically panchronic representation has dispelled feelings of "disorder" from an incongruous surface-system. The temptation of giving bygone forms and ephemerous historical rules a pseudo-synchronic status was quite understandably strong, and these linguists came to use the technique of internal reconstruction as a descriptive method.[2]

---

[1] For instance, in the case of partial supplying, the rule that provides more "customers" to the other tends to precede (Kiparsky's "feeding order"), rather than follow and make the other rule miss opportunities (Kiparsky's "bleeding order").

[2] Naturally, it was sometimes impossible not to notice the discrepancy between the order of appearance of documented historical developments and the derivability from an underlying form through rules. See Halle 1962: 68 and Chomsky-Halle 1968: 256, 281, where it is held possible

The excessive use of the device of extrinsic ordering in linguistic descriptions has come under attack in recent work. Koutsoudas (1972) shows that in several cases where extrinsic ordering has been posited, the order of rules attested is a direct consequence of the order of appearance of the structural descriptions that trigger the application of these rules. Thus, these sequences are basically unordered (see (1a) and (1b) above). Koutsoudas concludes that until "one clear case in which a pair of rules must be extrinsically ordered" is demonstrated, he considers the assumption that "rules are unordered" (which also includes cases of intrinsic order) "a viable assumption concerning rule-ordering." Ringen (1972) suggests a requirement that "if a phrase-marker meets the structural description of both an optional and an obligatory rule, the obligatory rule must apply to that phrase-marker" (14), or in other terms, the obligatory-optional order is governed by a general principle that need not be listed in a particular grammar. If correct, this would invalidate some of the arguments for extrinsic ordering, but, as Ringen admits, does not prove that "no rules are extrinsically ordered" (3).

What these two articles aim to show is that many heretofore adduced examples of rule-ordering need no extrinsic ordering device used by the grammar of a particular language, but the order of application is a mere consequence of the facts, of the status of the rules. A much stronger position is adopted in Koutsoudas-Sanders-Noll (1971, chronologically subsequent to the other two). The main hypothesis advanced therein is:

(2) "All restrictions on the relative order of application of grammatical rules are determined by universal rather than language-specific principles, from which it follows that no grammatical rules are extrinsically ordered."

The universal principles imposing a natural order on rules, when needed, are the following two (reproducing, in a contracted shape, their (15) and (18)):

(3) For any representation R, which meets the structural descriptions of each of two rules A and B, A takes applicational precedence over B—

(a) if there is some string that is included in the inputs of both A and B but not in the output of B (Counter-Bleeding Precedence) or

(b) if and only if the structural description of A properly includes the structural description of B (Proper Inclusion Precedence).

In other words, the Counter-Bleeding Precedence principle (3a) says that in the event that a given representation is eligible for the application of two rules at the same time, if one of the rules does not alter that part of the string that qualifies it for either one of the rules to the extent that it would no longer be eligible, while the other does, the non-altering rule (which either affects adjacent elements only, or alters the qualifying portion only so that it would still qualify) will naturally apply before the other one. This principle is proposed by Koutsoudas et. al. only as an alternative to the idea of simultaneous application of the two rules for cases of Counter-Bleeding (when the second rule would diminish the number of applications of the first rule, were it to apply first). Cases of Bleeding-and-Counter-Bleeding (when, in addition, the actual order also decreases the number of applications of the second rule), on the other hand,

---

that some rules are added in positions other than the end of the subdivision of the grammar they are referring to (though the general tendency is to add at the end). This increases the power of historical rule-addition to safeguard the panchronic principle. Moreover, Chafe (1968: 129) pointed out that unlike diachrony, a synchronic system allows simultaneous ordering (my (1a) above), and minimizes the degrees of depth. Yet this compromise still advocates partial preservation of historical events in a synchronic system.

are handled by the Proper Inclusion Precedence (3b) which says that for a given string, a special rule with a more restricted contextual definition must precede a general one which refers to a wider, less specific context, theoretically including the more specific one.[1] This is logical. The other order, with the general rule first, would drive the special rule out of existence. In other words, when the two possible orders offer moderate blood-sucking vs. bleeding to death, the first, more humane alternative is selected. It so happens that the non-viability of the first rule, were it second, is also true for all but one example of Counter-Bleeding mentioned by Koutsoudas et al. where (3a) is supposed to apply. The only exception is the case of Uruguayan Spanish having a sequence of rules $e \rightarrow \epsilon\ /\ \_\_C$, $s \rightarrow \phi\ /\ \_\_\#$, for a derivation klases → klasɛs → klasɛ (clases 'classes'), where the first rule would still have applications even if it were ordered after the second. I wonder, however, whether it is legitimate at all to posit a final -s for plural in the underlying representation of this dialect (just to make it similar to Castilian). For that matter, this line of argument can be applied to many other examples in Koutsoudas et al. 1971.

With the exception just mentioned, it appears that the idea underlying both principles (3a) and (3b) is that if the existence of a given rule can be stated in a given language, it has to precede any other eventual rule which, as far as its effect is concerned, would wipe out all the contexts qualifying for the first rule (cf. (1c, i) above).

These two principles make good sense. It is another question whether they can take care of all the cases where the relative ordering of two rules is crucial for the production of correct surface expressions. Koutsoudas et al. (1971) are often (though not always) successful in showing that orderings hitherto believed to be extrinsic are properly intrinsic. Directing their criticism mainly against Kiparsky 1968, they show that several cases of putative reordering of rules are in reality changes of rules.[2] Another principle used by them is that some rules would create a bundle of features which correspond to a phoneme unattested in that language or dialect, so that an adjustment rule must automatically apply. (Of course, one might wonder why these languages did not develop a new phoneme here). There could be a much stronger point of criticism against most of Kiparsky's cases of reordering, already suggested by Chafe (1968: 131, against Kiparsky 1968: 199-200), namely that these changes are properly changes in the underlying form. As already mentioned, many of these cases depend on an overly abstract underlying representation, still the same as the surface form in some older stage of the language, and not supported by any direct surface manifestation in the stage described (cf. page 10, fn. 1); this practice is highly objectionable.

A likewise extreme position was adopted by Vennemann who has defined his version of "natural generative grammar" as "a generative theory of language which is characterized primarily by the absence of a provision for extrinsic rule ordering" (1972: 110).

In the following, having tentatively accepted the principles suggested by Koutsoudas et. al. ((3) above), I am first proposing, not without reservations, another possible principle of universal rule-ordering, then I show that the device of extrinsic ordering itself, within strict limits, is still needed in linguistic theory. There are cases where it is the most efficient and realistic representational technique.

---

[1] This is closely akin to the principle of decreasing specificity of environments suggested for the disjunctive ordering of allomorph-spelling rules in Hetzron 1972a.

[2] I myself plead guilty of not admitting this, in Hetzron 1972b, 3.3 (originally written in summer 1970). First of all, the overly abstract underlying representation of the definiteness morpheme is unrealistic. Secondly, the simplification of the restriction on the assimilation rule $t + y \rightarrow \check{c}$ (etc.), cf. ibid., fn. 25, seems to me now to be sufficient justification for the change. Consequently, no reordering of rules is needed for accounting for the change described.

2. ARABIC: LONG VOWELS IN CLOSED SYLLABLES

2.1 CLASSICAL ARABIC

The following is a case in Classical Arabic where the most efficient ordering of rules seems to be extrinsic in that it cannot be explained by any of the general principles hitherto advanced, nor is it a "natural" order.

In Classical Arabic, with one type of exception to be dealt with below, long vowels appear in open syllables only. Underlying long vowels in a closed syllable undergo vowel-shortening (see Fischer 1969: 66). The examples are:

(4)	(a)	*yamu:t	→	yamut	'let him die!'
	(a')	yamu:tu:			'let them die!'
	(b)	*ama:tta	→	amatta	'you caused to die'
	(b')	ama:ta			'he caused to die'

The assumption that (a) and (b) have underlying long vowels can be substantiated by respective comparison with (a') and (b'), where the forms listed are members of the same paradigm as the ones above them. These examples show that in an open syllable, where both long and short vowels are permitted, the vowel is long in these cases; whereas in a closed syllable, which is created either by a word-final position (4a) or by the addition of a suffix beginning with a consonant (4b), and where only short vowels are allowed and length is thus neutralized, the vowel becomes short. The vowel shortening can be formally represented by the following rule:

(5) Vowel-shortening

$$V{:} \rightarrow \breve{V} \,/\, \_\_C \begin{Bmatrix} C \\ \# \end{Bmatrix}$$

i.e., a long vowel becomes short when preceding either two consonants or one consonant in word-final position.[1]

Let us now examine another set of facts. In verbal roots of the pattern 1-2-2 (mediae geminatae, where the second and third radicals are the same consonant), the two identical consonants may be contracted. Here are the examples, based on the root š-d-d:

(6)	(a)	*šadada	→	šadda	'he attacked/tightened'
	(b)	*yašdudu	→	yašuddu	'he attacks/tightens'
	(c)	yašdud (unaltered)	~ (→)	yašuddi	'let him attack/tighten!'
	(d)	šadadta			'you attacked/tightened'
	(e)	šaddada			'he strengthened' (unaltered, II form)
	(f)	šu:dida			'he was persecuted' (unaltered, passive of III form)

[1] Such shortening does not take place, if the long vowel is open: a:, before the energetic suffix -nni (itself the result of a dissimilation from -nna after a:), see Wright 1967, I § 97: dual yaktuba:nni 'they both will surely write', fem. pl.: yaktubna:nii 'they [fem.] will surely write', cf. masc. pl.: yaktubunna 'they [masc.] will surely write' (from yaktubu:+nna).

Again, the underlying forms, asterisked in (a) and (b), are fully justified by the general patterning of verbs other than 1-2-2. The contraction takes place in (a) and (b), optionally in (c), but not in (d) and (e). These facts can be represented by the following rule:

(7) 2-2 Contraction

$$\begin{array}{cccccc} \begin{Bmatrix} \langle C_j \rangle \\ X \end{Bmatrix} & C_i & \breve{V} & C_i & \begin{Bmatrix} (\#) \\ V \end{Bmatrix} & \\ 1 & 2 & 3 & 4 & 5 & \rightarrow \\ 1\ \langle 3 \rangle & 2 & \emptyset & 4 & 5 & \end{array}$$

where 2 and 4 are the last two radicals of a root,[1] and 1 ≠ u:; optional when 5 = #.

The rule says that a short vowel surrounded by two identical consonants that constitute the last two radicals of a root, if it is further the center of an open syllable (5 = V) or, optionally only, in a final closed syllable, is subject to one of the following changes: in the event that the first instance of identical consonants is further preceded by another consonant (1 = C_j, but not by the same consonant forming a geminate (6e)), the short vowel recedes and is inserted between these two consonants: (6b) and optionally in (6c) (this eventuality is indicated by the angle brackets); otherwise, unless the first identical consonant is preceded by a long u:[2] (6f), the short vowel is simply deleted: (6a). In both cases, recession of the vowel in (6b–c) or its deletion (6a), the joining of the two identical consonants into a geminate has been achieved.

There are cases where the two rules, the Vowel-Shortening (5) and the 2-2 Contraction (7) are in conflict: when, in the underlying pattern, the first identical consonant is preceded by a long a: (1 = a: in (7)). Such cases are, for example, the active participle of the I form and the active counterpart of (6f):

(8)	(a)	*ša:did^{un}	→	ša:dd^{un}	'the attacking/tightening one'
	(b)	ša:dada	→	ša:dda	'he persecuted' (III form)

The asterisked left side of (8a) is perfectly justified by the general patterns and the left side of (8b) is actually attested (cf. page 7, fn. 1). The right sides, on the other hand, the actual forms attested on the surface, contain a long vowel in a closed syllable, rendered closed by the application of the 2-2 Contraction rule (7). Thus, only this Contraction rule applied to the underlying forms in (a-b), and they were left intact by the Vowel-shortening rule (5).

The most efficient way of representing the fact that the long vowel *may* exceptionally appear in closed syllables created by the 2-2 Contraction rule is to order the Vowel-shortening rule *before* the Contraction, so that when the Contraction applies, the Vowel-shortening is no more actual:

---

[1] Or the reduplicated last radicals of the so-called IX and XI forms of the verb. Otherwise, identical consonants separated by a short vowel *are* possible: yutatabbiʕu 'he follows'. In the III and VI forms (after long a:) the contraction sometimes does not take place, see Brockelmann 1965, §45d. In Hebrew, the contraction could take place also when there was a long vowel between the identical consonants, see Halper 1910: 52.

[2] This u: can also be specified as a long closed vowel, since no i: is attested in this position.

(9) Underlying forms:	*ama:tta	*šadada	ša:dada
(i) Vowel-shortening:	amatta	————	————
(ii) 2-2 Contraction:	————	šadda	ša:dda

First, the Vowel-shortening rule is given a chance to operate. The underlying form ša:dada is not subject to it, since, at this stage, its long vowel is still in an open syllable. Then, the 2-2 Contraction rule is introduced, and the result is ša:dda which, this late, is no more eligible for Vowel-shortening. This seems to be an example of clear extrinsic ordering. This is what Koutsoudas et. al. (1971) would call a Counter-Feeding order, in that (ii) could supply new "customers" for (9i) if they had the opposite relative order; but they do not. The unmarked order would be "2-2 Contraction + Vowel-shortening," since the contraction rule is a closed-syllable-creating device, leading to a configuration that appears in the Structural Description of the input of Vowel-shortening. Nevertheless, such a "natural" ordering would create the incorrect form *šadda from underlying ša:dada. The most reasonable solution to this problem is apparently to attach to the rules number-tags indicating order of application, number-tags that are not defined by the universal principles hitherto proposed, but inferred from empirical evidence. And this is what extrinsic ordering is all about.

Before going on, let me mention one more similar, though rather marginal, case. The interrogative particle ʔa- preceding the Sg.1c. verbal prefix ʔa- may also be contracted with it (i.e., the intervening glottal stop is dropped), and the long vowel thereby created is not shortened, even though it may find itself to be the center of a closed syllable (Brockelmann 1965: §10f.) *ʔaʔadxulu → ʔa:dxulu 'shall I enter?'. This is a further contraction rule that is supposed to follow the Vowel-shortening rule (5) ~ (9i).

2.2 AN EXCEPTION TO THE RULE?

Is there any other way to represent this situation? The traditional description, as exemplified by Wright 1967 (I, §§13, 25) and Brockelmann 1965 (§11b), states that closed syllables contain only short vowels, except when the subsequent consonant is a geminate, and other [underlying] long vowels are shortened in closed syllables. As we have seen in (4b), being followed by a geminate is no sufficient specification for long vowels surviving in a closed syllable. The geminate must represent the second and third radicals of a root. Furthermore, the last paragraph of 2.1 shows a case of long vowel before a non-geminate consonant cluster. The permitted occurrence of long vowels in closed syllables can thus be more precisely defined as either being before a contracted geminate or arising from a contraction of vowels. This could be represented as follows:

(10) (i) Contractions ($C_iVC_i \rightarrow C_i$: or ʔaʔa → ʔa:)

(ii) Long Vowel shortening in closed syllables except when this situation has been created by a contraction as in (i)

These two rules are automatically ordered with relation to each other. Stating the exception in (10ii) presupposes earlier execution of the contraction (10i). This is an intrinsic order automatically following from the way the rules are formulated (Chomsky 1965: 223, fn. 6). The actual order is, in this formulation, the opposite of what we find under (9).

The inelegance of (10) is quite obvious. It is, in a sense, repetitious, since it refers to contractions in two instances, once as an instruction for execution: (10i), and once as an exception, a constraint on the execution of another rule: (10ii). Such a representation has been felt to be undesirable by many linguists. According to Hjelmslev's "empirical principle" (1961: 11), "The description shall be free of contradiction (self-consistent), exhaustive, and as simple as possible."

The first two requirements (self-consistency, exhaustiveness) are satisfied by both (9) and (10), but (9) is definitely simpler than (10). The idea of "order of application" is present in both, but whereas in (9) the order is part of the basic descriptive data, (10) requires the statement of an "exception" from which the order automatically, and secondarily, follows. Simple rules and one given indication of order (extrinsic) as in (9) seem to me preferable to more complicated rules where double reference to the same phenomenon is the price to be paid for making the order a mere consequence of other facts, instead of a basic datum.

The principle of economy of descriptive rules was even more categorically stated by Halle (1962: 55): "Given two alternative descriptions of a particular body of data, the description containing fewer such symbols [that appear as the operative elements of a rule, R. H.] will be regarded as simpler and will, therefore, be preferred over the other." The number of actual symbols may be the same in (9) and (10), but they more frequently occur in (10). One description, (9), has to use the device of e x t r i n s i c o r d e r i n g, and the other, (10), the notion of e x c e p t i o n. While "order" (extrinsic) is a superimposed concept, an "exception" weakens the very formulation of a rule; it cripples it in a manner that seems arbitrary on the level of that rule. Both descriptions have to make use of order (which is inevitably inherent in the line-by-line presentation anyhow), but (9) presents it straightforwardly, whereas (10) makes use of the concept of exception in order to make a number of principles for intrinsic ordering also valid here. We have two artifices, one in each presentation, one directly saying what it means: extrinsic ordering, and one being introduced in order to suggest something else: the exception meant to order the exception-producing rule before the one containing the exception. This is obviously inelegant. The general principles for intrinsic rule-ordering would be efficient as a generalization if they were immediately applicable and would not depend on the intermediary artifice of "exceptions."

Yet, in all fairness, one may wonder whether the empirical principle of simplicity is really legitimate. They may represent an esthetically or otherwise motivated prejudice of the describer. There may exist more important criteria to be taken into account, criteria that may overrule the principle of "convenience for the describer." Such a criterium may be psychological (as brought up by Theo Vennemann in an informal conversation): the speaker performs the vowel-shortening in (4a): *yamu:t → yamut 'let him die!', etc., but at the moment he encounters a form like ša:ddun (8a), he is still aware of the fact that the geminate that puts the long vowel into a closed syllable represents the second and third radicals of the root, and for this reason he lets the vowel remain long in the spirit of the exception formulated in (10ii). Thus, the duplication of the mention of contractions in (10) may be psychologically justified, since the speaker, after having executed the contraction, is not supposed to "forget" between then and the surface that such a contraction has been performed.

2.3 LATER DEVELOPMENTS

In answer to this last argument I intend to show here that the Vowel-shortening rule (5) had no psychological reality at all in Arabic. In Hetzron 1972a I have shown that morphophonemic rules that lead to the diversification of paradigms (either to the creation of new paradigms within one inflected morphological category, or to the non-uniformity of forms within a given paradigm) do not necessarily have psychological reality after the time when the diversification actually takes place, i.e., when the older, more uniform, situation is just about to be disrupted. At all other times, only paradigms are real, and not the rules that produce them. Here, I am trying to prove the same point along the same line of reasoning. Let us assume, for the moment, that the following operations took place in Classical Arabic:

(11)	(a)	*yamu:t →	yamut	'let him die!' (VOWEL-SHORTENING)
cf.	(b)	yamu:tu		'he dies' (not subject to Vowel-shortening)
	(c)	*yašdudu →	yašuddu	'he tightens/attacks' (2-2 CONTRACTION)
cf.	(d)	yašdud		'let him tighten/attack!' (not subject to 2-2 Contraction)

In its later developments, Arabic lost its final short vowels. Thus, an original yaktubu 'he writes' became yaktub, with further modification of the vowels. Moreover, Jussive forms like (11a, d) or yaktub 'let him write!' completely disappeared from the dialects.

If there had been a psychologically real Vowel-shortening rule (5) throughout the Classical period of Arabic, (11b) yamu:tu, after losing its final -u (which was a change in the underlying representation) and having become yamu:t, should have immediately been eligible for the Vowel-shortening rule and become *yamut (like the Classical Jussive, see (11a)). Yet, this is not what happened. The length was not reduced following the fall of the final -u. The presently attested forms are all continuations of yamu:t, with the long vowel. This means that the Vowel-shortening rule was not active in that period. Even though the Classical situation was still describable in terms of environments, when these environments changed (here: a penultimate open syllable in yamu:tu became closed final: yamu:t), the surface-manifestation of the long vowel was not readjusted. The Vowel-shortening rule, being inactive, did not intervene.

The inactive character of the Vowel-shortening is a fact also for the true Classical period, well before the general loss of final short vowels. All through the history of Classical Arabic, sentence-final short vowels were dropped (Wright 1967, II § 224), yet triggering no shortening of a long vowel that may have thereby become the center of a closed syllable.

Note that in modern Arabic dialects one does find clearcut instances of vowel-shortening within the same paradigms. For instance, Cairene has the following length-reduction rule (cf. Mitchell 1962: 21):

(12) $$V: \rightarrow \breve{V} / \left\{ \begin{matrix} [\ \overline{\text{-stress}}\ ] \\ \_\_CC \end{matrix} \right\}$$

Examples: manadíil 'handkerchief' + -ha 'her' → manadílha, šá:did 'pulling' + -hum 'them' → šadídhum. Yet, Cairene needs a restriction on the distribution of underlying long vowels that Classical Arabic does not have: long vowels occur only in stressed syllables that are either open or singly closed final (-V:C#), and (12) operates only when the addition of a suffix modifies this. Furthermore, (12) is different in shape from the Classical Vowel-shortening rule (5). Thus, there is no historical continuity between (5) and (12), the latter is a later innovation.[1]

Let us now turn to the 1-2-2 verbs. At the first glance one might think that this is comparable to the case of the Vowel-shortening: when the underlying indicative form *yašdudu (11c) became *yašdud through loss of the final short vowel, it should have disqualified itself for the Contraction and remained yašdud, like the Classical Jussive (11d). Yet this is not what we find. The attested forms in modern Arabic are all descended from yašudd, with a final geminate. This seems to be an argument against the reality of underlying *yašdud + (u → ∅).

[1] The relative youth of (12) may also be confirmed by the fact that it still represents a psychologically real process. This can be learned from an astute observation by Mitchell (1962: 22). He notes that "a vowel which is generally short and corresponds to a long vowel in related forms is sometimes pronounced very long when the word containing it is singled out for emphasis, e.g., di γáalya gíddan! 'that's terribly dear!', cf. the more usual γálya (masc. γáali)." That is, for emphasis, the length-reduction rule (12) may be omitted, and the underlying length is brought to the surface. Note that in the application of (12) the underlying form is not abstract. A real form (the Masculine) is modified, here by the addition of the feminine marker -a (leading to the elision of the vocalic feature of i, thereby closing the preceding syllable), and in the examples above, by the addition of a suffix beginning in a consonant and/or modifying the position of the stress.

But there is an alternative explanation. Let us remember that already Classical Arabic allowed Contraction optionally also in final position, e.g., the alternation yašdud (uncontracted) ~ yašuddi (with an added final vowel to avoid word-final gemination, (6c)). Thus, the new indicative yašudd could be attributed to taking the option already pre-existing in the Classical system (and the new system tolerates final geminates). However, the change was more radical. Classical šadadta (Past Sg.2m, (6d)), with a consonant after the critical syllable, was not eligible for Contraction. The elimination of the final short vowels would yield *šadadt for modern Arabic. The form actually attested is šadde:t, with a Contraction even in this configuration, and with an added anaptyctic -e:- after the new geminate.[1] How can this extension of the Contraction to pre-consonantal positions be explained?[2] Naturally, this was a levelling operation: in the entire finite conjugation there was no more any instance of separation between the two identical consonants (while in the non-finite system, there was still mašdu:d, a passive participle, 'pulled'; for the active participle, see below). But what triggered it?

Let us compare the Classical 2-2 Contraction rule and the Modern one:

(13) (a) Classical $\left\{\begin{matrix}\langle C_j\rangle \\ X\end{matrix}\right\} C_i\check{V}C_i \left\{\begin{matrix}(\#) \\ V\end{matrix}\right\} \rightarrow \left\{\begin{matrix}\langle C_j\check{V}\rangle \\ X\end{matrix}\right\} C_iC_i \left\{\begin{matrix}(\#) \\ V\end{matrix}\right\}$

(b) Modern $\left\{\begin{matrix}\langle C_j\rangle \\ X\end{matrix}\right\} C_i\check{V}C_i \rightarrow \left\{\begin{matrix}\langle C_j\check{V}\rangle \\ X\end{matrix}\right\} C_iC_i$ with limitations[3]

where $\check{V}$ stands for the same vowel and $X \neq u$:

The main difference between (13a) and (13b) is the final slot. The Classical language limits the rule according to the status of the syllable with the doomed vowel, whereas the Modern dialects do not. One can see that (13b) logically follows from (13a). Most of the occurrences of V were word-final and they came to disappear. Thus, the applicability of the rule in final syllables (-#) was extended to this case, with an obligatory force. This reorganization of the post-C_iVC_i slot led to a complete elimination of its relevance. Even the specification # was dropped, and the Contraction was extended to all instances of C_iVC_i, and in the event that it was followed by a consonant, a palatal vowel was added to the new geminate. This actual extension indicates that the 2-2 Contraction rule, in its innovated shape (13b) was well and alive when the Classical system started to break down. Let us add, as a possible argument, that in Cairene and in the urban dialects of the large Syro-Palestino-Mesopotamian area, where (13b) could not apply after

---

[1] With a short vowel for Sg. 3f. in most dialects (šaddit/šaddät, for Classical šadadt), but long in the other persons. Usually the analogical influence of verbs with final radical y is evoked here in the grammars.

[2] Already some of the ancient dialects used Contraction for the entire past tense conjugation (Rabin 1951: 163-4), the type ẓiltu/ẓaltu for ẓaliltu 'I did all day' in Hijaz (while still uncontracted in madadna: 'we stretched' with an a between the identical consonants), and in the East (Bakr) raddatu 'I gave back' for radadtu. Rabin suspects here a pronunciation raddətu. The form radda:tu is also mentioned. This is reminiscent of Hebrew which has sabbo:ti 'I surrounded' with an o: corresponding to Arabic a:. Yet the modern forms are different in shape because of the adoption of a palatal vowel after the geminate (cf. page 11, fn. 1).

[3] Naturally, a single rule cannot embrace all the variety of modern Arabic dialects, but (13b) seems to be a relatively adequate generalization. In most dialects, (13b) is not valid for the III and VI forms (if attested at all for 1-2-2 verbs). For the urban dialects of the Syro-Palestino-Mesopotamian area, (13b) is not applied after any long a: (III, VI forms or active participles of I, see below), i.e., the condition ought to be $X \neq V{:}$.

long vowels at all (see page 11 fn. 3), for the masculine singular form of the active participle, form I, one finds š a : d i d, a revival of the underlying form in (8a), since the Contraction rule could no more apply. This seems to prove the psychological reality of the underlying form here.[1]

2.4 RECAPITULATION

Using historical arguments referring to the passage from Classical Arabic to later varieties, the direct ancestor(s) of the modern dialects, I have shown that the Vowel-shortening rule of Classical Arabic (5), was not productive anymore, since its effect was not felt when the changes occurred. On the other hand, the 2-2 Contraction rule, (7) ~ (13a → b) did take an active part in the reorganization of the system. This definitely discredits the psychological justification of the description using the concept of "exception": (10). If only the Contraction was a real process, it is quite clear that the other rule, the Vowel-shortening, had the status of merely being the linguist's construct, a deductive rule based on facts attested, and nothing more. In this case, one could not expect the latter to "operate" after the former, but one could very well expect the former, truly operative rule, Contraction, to act on a system that can be characterized by certain limitations on the syllabic structure (no long vowel in closed syllables), and when its action created a configuration contradicting this limiting condition, one could expect no repercussion from a nonproductive rule. This is precisely the ordering represented by (9).

2.5 THE PRODUCTIVITY PRINCIPLE

On the basis of these arguments one might suggest a further general principle of natural and and universal ordering, according to which in a linguistic description a n o n p r o d u c t i v e r u l e a l w a y s p r e c e d e s a l i v i n g, o p e r a t i v e o n e. This is a principle with psychological inspiration. The idea behind it is that some rules do not have an active status, they are only inferred from the facts by the linguist or, eventually, by the sophisticated speaker. They represent regularities in the system that can be detected after examination. Other rules, on the other hand, are true, active, productive operations that are real parts of the speaker's competence. For instance, a speaker of English may very well notice the regularity in the case of sing/sang/sung, also found in sink/sank/sunk, but this is a highly limited regularity and unlikely to have true psychological existence. The speaker has to know these forms as part of his knowledge of the vocabulary, and no putative rule i → a . . . is necessary for him. On the other hand, the realizations of plural/genitive/present Sg. 3. ending -s as [-s], [-z], [-iz] according to the environment most probably represent a true operation, an adjustment made at the time the form is produced.

In the case of the Arabic Vowel-shortening, its psychological non-reality throughout history is made probable by the fact that the deletion of sentence-final short vowels did not trigger it (see above, in 2.3). The psychological reality of the 2-2 Contraction in the transitional period between Classical and pre-Modern is evidenced by the fact that š a d a d t a was replaced by š a d d e : t, i.e. the contraction was extended to a pre-consonant position, (13a)~(13b), and by the reviving of the underlying form of the active participle š a : d i d in some dialects (but not in most of them, see page 12, fn. 1). Strictly speaking, this, in itself, still does not prove that the 2-2 Contraction rule was kept alive throughout the history of Arabic (e.g. the active participle š a : d i d could easily be a reconstruction on the basis of the regular pattern).

[1] Cf. Feghali 1919: 155-6. The other dialects have corresponding forms š a : d d / š a : d, or more rarely š á d d i / š ó d d (Central Asia). According to Halper 1910: 49-50, one of the alternatives for Hebrew was of the last type, with further degemination, *s a : b i b → s o : ƀ e ƀ or → *s a : b b → *s a b b → s a ƀ. It is interesting that some Arabic dialects have no active participle form I for 1-2-2 verbs, as if to avoid "embarrassing" phonetic configurations.

Instead of drawing a categorical conclusion, let me sum up the above as follows. It is possible that the productive/non-productive character of the rules may serve as a universal ordering principle: the productive rule follows the non-productive one. The difficulty in testing this proposal is that the productive character of a morphophonemic rule is hard to verify. Tentatively, we can state that there is likelihood for the reality of such a rule when the underlying form is not abstract but is also attested in the surface system of the language. Such a case is that of the Cairene Arabic length-reduction rule(12) which operates only when a suffix is added to a basic form capable of standing alone (cf. page 10, fn. 1). For the Classical contracted forms, e.g. yašuddu (6b), the interparadigmatic coexistence of a regular yaktubu 'he writes' makes the underlying *yašdudu psychologically plausible, but the intraparadigmatic co-existence of a yamu:tu: (4a') does not seem to be sufficient justification for a psychologically underlying *yamu:t for surface yamut (4a). Does this mean that the coexistence of a regular paradigm helps to keep the underlying (regular) forms of an irregular paradigm psychologically real, whereas the coexistence of a basic form and a "modified" one in the same paradigm does not? Or is the reason that yamut is a shorter form, that ought to be basic, hence it cannot be considered derived? To answer these questions, a large number of examples should be examined.

3. ARABIC NUMERAL AGREEMENT

In this section I shall present a case where extrinsic ordering should be a part of the active system of language, i.e., the agreement rules, the psychological reality and operational character of which can hardly be denied.

Koutsoudas et. al. (1971: 2) listed nine theoretically possible relationships between ordered rules according to the quantitative effect the output of one has on the potential or real input of the other. One of these relationships is labelled "Mutually non-affecting" where, given a sequence of rules A-B, A neither increases nor decreases the number of forms to which B applies on the one hand, and, on the other, if the order were B-A, there would be no increase or decrease occasioned by B affecting the width of application of A either. They further say (16): "Since the outputs of mutually non-affecting rules have no effect on their respective inputs, there can be no possible empirical consequence of different orders of application." What they have overlooked is that by "effect" they only mean "quantitative effect," and there can be cases where the effect is strictly qualitative, without affecting quantity.

In the following, I shall present a case where there is a rule A affecting X in the environment of Y, followed by a rule B affecting Y in the environment of X. X is a value-marked category, so that the input of B will not be quantitatively affected by the outcome of A, but since A will change the value of X, it will have a clear qualitative effect on B. For this reason, the order must strictly be A-B. A possible order B-A (which once probably existed) would command exactly the same number of applications for each rule, but it would yield the wrong results. This is the case of the numeral agreement in Classical Arabic.

3.1 FACTS

In Classical Arabic (as in the classical Semitic languages in general) the numerals 3-19 agree in gender with the subsequent noun. A peculiar feature of this agreement is that the numerals 3-10 having an ending -at elsewhere known as a feminine-marker actually co-occur with masculine nouns and are consequently descriptively masculine, and the same numerals lacking this ending, i.e. having the external appearance of a masculine, are paired with feminine nouns:

(14) (a) θala:θat^{u} tala:miðat^{in} 'three [male or mixed] students [pl]'

(b) θala:θ^{u} tilmi:ða:t^{in} 'three [female] students [pl]'

This phenomenon is traditionally called incongruence. For a historical explanation of the origin of this incongruence, see Hetzron 1967. Syntactically, on the other hand, there is no problem in classifying numerals in -at as masculine, and without it as feminine.[1]

There is, on the other hand, a real difficulty as far as the syntax of the Arabic numeral agreement is concerned. In the Arabic noun-system, all the plurals of nonhumans are feminine singulars in the agreement rules referring to pronouns, adjectives, and verbs:

(15) (a) kutub^{un} kabi:rat^{un} 'large books'

(cf. kita:b^{un} kabi:r^{un} 'a large book')

(b) mudun^{un} kabi:rat^{un} 'large towns'

(cf. madi:nat^{un} kabi:rat^{un} 'a large town')

The examples show that both plurals, independently of the gender of the corresponding singular (masculine for 'book' and feminine for 'town'), are treated as feminine singulars and require the feminine singular adjective kabi:rat- 'large' (masc.sg. kabi:r-, pl. kiba:r-).

If one examines the combination of such nouns with numerals, one finds that the agreement rules operate differently from the case above:

(16) (a) θala:θat^{u} kutub^{in} kabi:rat^{in} 'three [masc.] large books [fem.sg.]'

(b) θala:θ^{u} mudun^{in} kabi:rat^{in} 'three [fem.] large towns [fem.sg.]'

This shows that the two plural nouns, kutub- and mudun-, which have exactly the same feminine singular status in the agreement rules with adjectives, as illustrated by (15) or the last words in (16), do not have the same standing vis-à-vis the numerals. Kutub- requires the masculine numeral θala:θat- because the corresponding singular: kita:b- is a masculine, whereas mudun- is preceded by the feminine numeral θala:θ- as the corresponding singular: madi:nat- is a feminine. This can be formulated in the following manner: the agreement between a numeral and a noun is always made on the basis of the underlying singular form of the noun, and not with the cooccurring plural. For humans, there is no change of gender between singular and plural, so that no conflict could arise.

3.2 FORMAL REPRESENTATION

As already illustrated in the above examples, nouns following the numerals 3-10 have to be pluralized. The set of rules (17) can take care of the facts:[2]

---

[1] I have two reasons for mentioning incongruence here: to make the reader aware of the character of the feminine ending -at, and to hint at the fact that the historical origin of the extrinsic ordering mentioned below (17) is to be associated with the incongruence, cf. Hetzron 1967: 190.

[2] In view of the nightmarish complicatedness of the optional variations in the Arabic numeral agreement, I am disregarding all the variants that are not obtained in the most straightforward

(17)				
(i)	$\text{Numeral}_{3\text{-}19}$	→	$[\alpha \text{ masculine}]$ / ______	$\begin{bmatrix}\text{Noun}\\ \alpha\text{Masculine}\end{bmatrix}$
(ii)	Noun	→	$[-\text{singular}]$ /	$\text{Numeral}_{3\text{-}10}$ ______
(iii)	$\begin{bmatrix}\text{Noun}\\ -\text{human}\\ -\text{singular}\end{bmatrix}$	→	$\begin{bmatrix}-\text{masculine}\\ +\text{singular}\end{bmatrix}$	
(iv)	Other agreement rules			

In these rules, (17i) imposes on the numerals 3-19 the same gender as that of the subsequent noun. (17ii) pluralizes the nouns occurring after the numerals 3-10. (17iii) is a more general rule, applying to all nonhuman plurals, whatever the origin, and not only to the output of (17ii). It imposes on nonhuman plurals the features "feminine" and "singular" which, henceforth, will figure in the input of the other agreement rules: (17iv), yielding constructions like (15).

The relative ordering of the pluralization rule (17ii) and the gender/number-regulation rule (17iii) can be called "unmarked" (in (1d)). The other order is theoretically possible, since the two rules are not coextensive. Such an order would mean that quantified plurals (from (17ii)) and other plurals would behave differently in other agreement rules (17iv).

On the other hand, the structural descriptions of the numeral-agreement rule (17i) and the other agreement rules (17iv) contain references to features like [α masculine], [α singular]. It cannot be claimed that these rules are unordered in that they may apply whenever they encounter a combination of Noun (necessarily gender- and number-marked) and an agreeing element (numeral, adjective, pronoun, verb with subject). (17iii) is a gender/number-regulating rule which necessarily alters the number and eventually also the gender. It matters a great deal whether agreement rules apply before or after it. The most natural position for all such agreement rules is after (17iii). This may be formulated in the shape of a general principle, more limited in scope but comparable in status to (3), in the spirit of (2): *agreement rules start operating when the categories involved have assumed their definite status*. Yet, while (17iv) conforms to this intuitively justified principle, (17i), the numeral agreement, constitutes a counterexample. If this agreement-rule also followed the gender/number-regulating rule (17iii), one would obtain ungrammatical constructions like *θala:θ^{u} kutub^{in} (Num: fem., Noun: fem.-through-pluralization) instead of the correct form: (16a) θala:θat^{u} kutub^{in}. This one can be produced only by extrinsically ordering (17i) before (17iii).[1]

---

manner. These variations are the following. Broken plural (= a plural form obtained through internal vocalic modifications) of humans is sometimes treated as non-human in (17iii). Adjectives sometimes agree with the numeral instead of the noun, in which case an expression like (16a) would also have kabi:r^{un}. Note that this is not an agreement with the underlying singular, for it occurs in conjunction with numerals only, and not in (15a). And the most puzzling variation of all (Wright 1967, II, § 10), forms like ʿišru:na di:na:r^{an} na:ṣiriy:at^{an} 'twenty [no gender indicated] dinars [masc. sg.] of al-Malik an-Nasir [a fem. sg. adjective]', where the feminine singular adjective appears as if the noun were pluralized dana:ni:r^{u} (though after 20 it is not). This could be taken care of by an optional rule that makes all Num + Noun groups a plural. It is also possible to use here a masc. sg. adjective na:ṣiriy:^{an} in perfect agreement with di:na:r^{an}, the actual form. See also Reckendorff 1921: 206 for iθnata:ni waʔarbaʿu:na ḥalu:bat^{an} su:d^{an} 'forty-two black milking camels' ('two [fem] and-forty milking-camels [fem. sg.] black [pl]'), where one may also use sawda:ʔ^{a} 'black [fem. sg.]'. The omission of these variants from the discussion only means not mentioning certain optional rules or optional conditions on rules, and does not affect the main issues at all.

[1] There is one point worth mentioning. Koutsoudas et. al.'s Proper Inclusion Precedence

3.3 THE ALTERNATIVE

Is there any other way to represent the agreement of the Arabic numeral with the gender of the underlying singular of the co-occurring noun? One such way (proposed in an informal conversation by John Callender) is to posit the existence of a carried-over feature which, in the plural, still preserves a memory of the gender of the singular. This would involve something like the following:

(18) (i) Pluralization of nouns after 3-10 (= 17ii)

(ii) Gender/number regulation for nonhuman plurals (~ 17iii):

$$\begin{bmatrix} \text{Noun} \\ \text{-human} \\ \text{-singular} \end{bmatrix} \rightarrow \begin{bmatrix} \text{+feminine} \\ \text{+singular} \end{bmatrix}$$

(iii) Numeral gender-agreement rule sensitive to [α masculine]

(iv) Other agreement rules sensitive to [β feminine] [γ singular]

The difference between (17iii) and (18ii) is that the former modifies the underlying gender of the noun ([α masculine] → [-masculine]), whereas the latter has no effect on the [+masculine] feature, but adds a [+feminine] to the same noun. This system, (18), contains only "natural" orders. (18iii) is unordered and may apply wherever it encounters a [+masculine] feature. (18iv) is intrinsically ordered after (18ii) since its input, [βfeminine], is created by (18ii), and this will automatically lead to the proper agreement with the definitive number, also created by (18ii). The two agreement rules at the end are unordered with relation to each other, in the sense of (1a). (18ii) is actually ordered after (18i), but this is an unmarked order, and if order is not specified for either of them, the one indicated above would automatically be adopted. In other words, if (18ii) is only specified to apply to plural nonhuman nouns, one actually expects to apply it to the output of (18i) also, and if it were n o t so, that should be specially indicated.

---

principle (3b), as I understand it, mainly refers to linear inclusion, the sequence XY including X. It possibly also refers to vertical inclusion: features A and B cooccurring in the same segment include the occurrence of A only. Yet linguistic representation may be tridimensional, the third dimension being the set of elements that may alternately occur in the same slot. When comparing (17i) and (17ii) one finds that the former has a set of numerals (3-19) that p a r a d i g m a t i c a l l y includes the numerals listed in (17ii), 3-10. In other words, the numerals 11-19 that do receive gender-agreement by virtue of (17i) do not impose the plural on the subsequent noun, as the other numerals do. Yet this does not fall within the limits of (3b). The Precedence principles of (3) seem to be based on the idea that the other order of application would completely blot out rule A, since B would alter all of A's potential inputs. Here, in the case of the paradigmatic inclusion, this would not be the case.

From another angle, one may wonder whether (17i) is not ordered before (17ii)-(17iii) to prevent numerals of different gender from being used with the same noun: the gender of the plural for 3-10 and the gender of the singular for 11-19. The precedence of (17i) assures that a given noun always gets the same gender of numerals, whatever the numeral. In answer to this, one might first say that it is questionable whether the same gender of numerals can be considered an important principle when there are different genders of adjectives, etc., with the same noun according to number. Secondly, there is historical evidence indicating that when the order indicated in (17) was established, (17i) still referred to the numerals 3-10, i.e. was coextensive with (17ii), cf. Hetzron 1967: 192.

As it stands, (18) is incomplete. Within the scope of the present inquiry, it takes care of the combination "Numeral $_{3-10}$ + Plural Nonhuman Noun" only, but it does not account for numerals from 11 up, where the noun remains a singular (and acquires no [feminine] feature through (18ii) for which it is not eligible), nor for human nouns which maintain the same gender in the plural as in the singular (and are excluded from 18ii).

There are two possible ways to make (18) complete. One is to have a redundancy rule specify that all nouns that have not undergone (18ii) will get the feminine value opposite to the masculine. This putative rule must either be ordered before (18ii), so that the latter would modify the value of the already introduced feminine feature, or disjunctively after (18ii), so that it would no more modify an already introduced [+feminine] value. One can solve the ordering problem by using a prefix unmarked before [feminine]:

(19) $[\text{u feminine}] \rightarrow [-\alpha\,\text{feminine}] \;/\; [_{\alpha\,\text{masculine}}\overline{\quad\quad}]$

Since the output of (18ii) would have a marked value [+feminine], (19) could indifferently (cf. (1a)) apply before or after it.

Having solved this technical problem, let us see whether it was worth the effort. This alternative solution (18-19) generalizes the feature [+feminine], specifically invented for the conflicting case of "Numeral $_{3-10}$ + Nonhuman Noun," for the entire system. In reality, the putative feature [+feminine] is superfluous in most actual instances, i.e., in all the uses where it should be introduced by (19) and not (18ii): for all the singular, for all the plurals co-occurring with no numerals, for all the nouns appearing after numerals other than 3-10. This feature would be truly justified only for the minority of cases where there is a numeral of the latter type: 3-10. A rule like (19) is supposed to impose the standards established for a relatively insignificant minority on a reluctant and uninterested majority. Is then (19) anything more than a technical tour de force? From a mentalistic point of view, the speaker may very well feel some kind of duality in the specific configuration "Num $_{3-10}$ + Noun + other agreeing element," using one type of gender-specification for one purpose and another for other purposes, but it is absolutely unlikely that he will feel any kind of duality, be it of the trivial $-\alpha$type as in (19), in the other cases. The agreement of the numerals 3-10 with the noun is definitely something marked, evoking something that all the other cases do not have.

The other possible remedy to the incompleteness of (18) is to modify the agreement rules (18iv) so that in the absence of a [feminine] feature, the agreement can be imposed on the basis of the [masculine] feature (using, naturally, opposite value). This would be a disjunctive ordering:

(20) (~ (18iv), but only the portion referring to gender)

$$\text{Agreement-sensitive element} \rightarrow [\alpha\,\text{masculine}] \;/\; \left\{ \begin{matrix} [-\alpha\text{feminine}] \\ [\alpha\text{masculine}] \end{matrix} \right\}$$

where braces mark disjunctive ordering (cf. Hetzron 1972a, fn. 3), and no blank line appears in the environment specification to indicate that relative position of the agreement sensitive element and the agreement-imposing one is not relevant.

The disjunctive ordering of the two environments can be very well taken care of by the Proper Inclusion Principle of Sanders (18) in Koutsoudas et. all., (3b) above). According to (18), a [feminine]-containing segment must also contain a [masculine] feature, but not vice-versa. The first line of the environment, if more fully specified, is [+feminine] [+/-masculine], and the second line is only [+/-masculine], with no [feminine] feature at all. Thus, the environment of the first line properly includes that of the second.[1]

[1] A minor flaw of (20) is that it does not show that [feminine] can only be +, since it only

Let us compare this with (17), the set containing the extrinsic ordering. Either alternative solution, (18) - (19) with redundancy rule, or (18) - (20) with the modified agreement rule, makes use of one more feature ([α or +feminine]) than (17). It is thus uneconomical according to the criteria suggested by Halle (1962). Furthermore, the addition of another rule, (19), or the doubling of (20), makes the list of rules longer than in (17), thus disqualifying (18) from a Hjelmslevian point of view. But, as said above, one is entitled to question the validity of the simplicity criterium in evaluating competing representations.

Yet, one ought to realize that the above artifice, having separate [masculine] and [feminine] features, has been introduced for the sole reason that numerals that require plural nouns always agree with the underlying singular. Thus, neither version of (18) - (19)/(20) describes the observed and directly interpreted facts, but rather reflects a theoretical prejudice, deliberately introducing an artifice to *avoid* extrinsic ordering.

From a mentalistic point of view, one can argue as follows. The knowledge of the lexical gender, [±masculine], is part of the speaker's lexical competence. The feminine singular agreement with nonhuman plurals is located in the speaker's syntactic competence. We can thus oppose a constant gender and an occasionally superimposed one. The first is called [±masculine] in all the representations, and the second [-masculine] in (17), [+feminine] in (20) and it mingles with the constant gender under the label [+feminine] in (19). It is quite unlikely that the gender of the underlying singular [±masculine] will, for the speaker, be anything but the gender of the underlying singular, even in a configuration "Num_{3-10} + Nonhuman Noun." Either version (18) - (19)/(20) posits a bundle of features [±masculine] [+feminine] for all nonhuman plurals. [±masculine] will only be used in the minority of cases where there is a preceding numeral (3-10 only before a plural). While the [+feminine] is justified, in the speaker's mind, by the nonhuman plural character, an immediate datum, the other feature [±masculine] can only be justified if one goes *back* to the singular, or to the lexicon. Thus, this feature is definitely goverened by an *earlier*, static knowledge, whereas the [feminine] is an ad hoc imposition. This is already a mental ordering. In forms like *kutub-* 'books' (masc. in the sg.) and *mudun-* 'towns' (fem. in the sg.), the speaker will hardly feel the presence of another gender feature in addition to the feminine imposed by the plural. For the numeral agreements he will have recourse to the singular. It does not matter whether in any actual mental operation the execution of the numeral agreement precedes the pluralization, or after pluralization there is a flashback to the singular. Probably both possibilities are exploited on different occasions. The important point is that the numeral agreement will appear in the mind of the speaker with reference to the singular. He is always making the agreement with the underlying singular, referring to a pre-pluralization stage, and this is precisely what (17) says. Having a [±masculine] [+feminine] configuration in the spirit of (18) is expressing one thing by something else, calling the syntactic gender imposed on adjectives, verbs and pronouns [feminine], and calling the lexical gender, the earlier one still unaffected in the singular [masculine], instead of what it really is: the lexical gender. It is doubtful that in the mind of the speaker this ever becomes a separate syntactic marker, instead of remaining what it originally had been.

3.4 CONCLUSION

We can sum up the results of our reasoning as follows. If we do not adopt mentalisitc arguments in the evaluation of grammatical description, we are entitled to use whatever devices

---

appears in the output of (18ii). This can easily be remedied by reformulating (20) as follows:

$$\text{Agreeing element} \rightarrow \begin{bmatrix} [\text{-masc.}] \\ [\alpha\,\text{masc.}] \end{bmatrix} \;/\; \begin{bmatrix} [\text{+fem.}] \\ [\alpha\,\text{masc.}] \end{bmatrix}$$

we need for the shortest, simplest, exhaustive description, and (17) is definitely shorter and simpler than (18) (while both are exhaustive). Thus, extrinsic ordering is found to be advantageous in this framework, and this is enough justification. If on the other hand, we do try to use mentalistic arguments, expecting rules to have psychological correlates, we will still have to prefer (17) for being straightforward and for showing the true difference between an earlier (lexical) gender and a later (syntactically imposed) one, without trying to introduce intermediary devices that do not directly render and express the observed nature of the phenomena.

4. REFERENCES

Brockelmann, Carl. 1965. Arabische Grammatik. (Lehrbücher für das Studium der orientalischen und afrikanischen Sprachen, II) Leipzig: VEB Verlag Enzyklopädie.

Chafe, Wallace L. 1968 "The Ordering of Phonological Rules," International Journal of American Linguistics, 34. 115-36.

Chomsky, Noam. 1965. Aspects of the Theory of Syntax. Cambridge, Mass.: the M.I.T. Press.

Chomsky, Noam and Morris Halle. 1968. The Sound Pattern of English. New York: Harper and Row.

Feghali, Maurice T. 1919. Le parler arabe de Kfar 'abîda (Liban-Syrie). Paris: Leroux.

Fischer, Wolfdietrich. 1969. "Probleme der Silbenstruktur in Arabischen," in Proceedings of the International Conference on Semitic Studies, held in Jerusalem, 19-23 July, 1965. Jerusalem: The Israel Academy of Sciences and Humanities. 65-9.

Halle, Morris. 1962. "Phonology in Generative Grammar," Word, 18. 54-72.

Halper, B. 1910. "The participial formations of the geminate verbs," Zeitschrift für die alttestamentliche Wissenschaft, 30. 42-57, 99-126, 201-28.

Hetzron, Robert. 1967. "Agaw Numerals and Incongruence in Semitic," Journal of Semitic Studies, 12. 169-97.

__________ 1972a. "The Shape of a Rule and Diachrony," Bulletin of the School of Oriental and African Studies, 35. 451-75.

__________ 1972b. "Studies in Hungarian Morphophonology," Ural-Altaische Jahrbücher, 44. 79-106.

Hjelmslev, Louis. 1961. Prolegomena to a Theory of Language. Madison: University of Wisconsin Press.

Kiparsky, Paul. 1968. "Linguistic Universals and Linguistic Change," Emmon Bach and Robert T. Harms, eds. Universals in Linguistic Theory. New York: Holt, Rinehart and Winston. 171-202.

Koutsoudas, Andreas. 1972. "The Strict Order Fallacy," Language, 48. 88-96.

Koutsoudas, Andreas, Gerald Sanders and Craig Noll. 1971. "On the Application of Phonological Rules," Indiana University Linguistics Club.

Mitchell, T.F. 1962. Colloquial Arabic: The Living Language of Egypt. (The Teach Yourself Book). London: The English Universities Press.

Rabin, Chaim. 1951. Ancient West-Arabian. London: Taylor's Foreign Press.

Reckendorf, H. 1921. Arabische Syntax. Heidelberg: Winter.

Ringen, Catherine. 1972. "On Arguments for Rule Ordering." Foundations of Language, 8. 266-73.

Vennemann, Theo. 1972. "Phonological Uniqueness in Natural Generative Grammar," Glossa, 6. 105-16.

Wright, W. 1967. A Grammar of the Arabic Language. Translated from the German of Caspari and edited with numerous additions and corrections. Third edition revised by W. Robertson Smith and M.J. de Goeje (originally 1859-62[1], 1874[2], 1896-8[3]), Cambridge: The University Press.